Somewhere,
in front of my name

SAINT JULIAN PRESS

POETRY

Praise for *Somewhere, in front of my name*

In our current poetic landscape, Prosser Stirling defies the bland prosaic line with word painting, sound, and pace rarely found. This stunning first collection, *Somewhere, in front of my name*, has a great diversity of presentations; whether exploring a specific place, event, or abstract metaphor, all the poems contain a singular and immediate voice and style with superbly crafted orchestration and imagery. Stirling is a magician, with a steady flow of arresting passages keeping you on the page for rereading. It is poetry as it best and as it should be: the art of language.

—Mark Fishbein
Host of DC Poetry Collective
Chancellor of PGN-Poetry
Global Network's Poetry Academy

Prosser demonstrates his uncanny ability to find the perfect word or phrase. He has both an eye and an ear for the unusual, like a master riddle maker. The reader will find poems that contain nouns repurposed to verbs, as though the words have died and been resurrected to a new higher form of being. Alliteration is wisely used in much the same way a master chef knows just the right pinch of spices that make a dish divine.

As Billy Collins teaches, Prosser understands that the poem ends when the reader stops reading. In other words, each poem ends exactly where the reader is emotionally prepared for it to end. If this is your first venture into reading Prosser Stirling's work, be sure to snuggle up with a dictionary and hot cup of ginger tea. You'll need them both. I know you'll enjoy this book.

—Terry Jude Miller
Poet

Prosser Stirling's new collection of poems embarks upon the passionate river of existence with serene but wide-open eyes. It navigates readers through shifting currents while prodding the depths for profound meaning. "Slackened oars break the sound / as my skiff drifts in silver-plated wake; / between green growing on green, / ghosted cypress stumps, / stone solemn, / absorb the boat wash / to silence my passage." The poet always seems to be searching for something just out of reach – the cusp of connection, a sense memory, a singular understanding. Something loved, something lost, or something not yet dreamed. "I... take shelter under wattled withes, / and bird my way through fell acres to seek you, / still not knowing / your face / or name." Stirling's keen eye and ear are evident in compact and sound-rich lines fertile with implication. Every poem is a puzzle box. Sitting with it and pausing in the breath of the line break, fresh wisdom erupts. These poems marvel at the overtly awe-inspiring (the macro, the meta) as well as the wonders hidden in the micro and the trace. We can feel the cosmic gravity between all bodes, in all versions, that tread this earth... human and human, human and nature, human and his past. "Something big watches us / with animacy of an older world. / Is it a god being born / or two souls at eclipse, / about to detonate / from nearness?" Stirling invites us to dip our oars right along with him into the unknown. Together, we stir at the waters to find out more and more from this world we live in – about the bonds that tie us to one another, and to it.

—Dana Gittings
*The Dark Dance*

# Somewhere,
# in front of my name

Poems

by

## Prosser Stirling

SAINT JULIAN PRESS
HOUSTON

Published by
SAINT JULIAN PRESS, Inc.
2053 Cortlandt, Suite 200
Houston, Texas 77008

www.saintjulianpress.com

Paperback ISBN-13:  978-1-955194-33-4
eBook EPUB ISBN:  978-1-955194-34-1
Library of Congress Control Number:  2024939225

Cover Art Credit: Prosser Stirling
Author Photo Credit: Elliott O'Donovan

*for*

EPS

# CONTENTS

# Somewhere,
# in front of my name

# 1.
# Somewhere, in front of my name

## Night Vision

While hart and hare
lay still in their wood,
the two-toed dung beetle,
whose radar-domed eyes can see
where rainbows nap at night,
pays no heed
to raccoons under mask
on midnight haj.
Galloping down the path,
they slow to a ring-tail waddle
as he pushes his parcel to a stop.
The scarab's trowels then plow a pit
to roll the booty down.

Above, owls gable then dive—
a gentle waft of wing
is all that is heard
as the night widens.
Bashful skunk bears lower noses
to wander and wend their way;
a hangar of fruit bats,
cagey and kicky,
find feeling to fly,
then loiter for turns at nectar.

Heavy mosquitos,
high on their hosts,
stay pooled in loot.
In the fens where ducklings muddle,
unknown forms cat silently by,
then mink away with prize.

All let the beetle toil on,
unaware of his buried treasure,
passive to his iridescent glow,
the same that rainbows make tonight.

## Mare frigoris
*The Sea of Cold*

Women, high-wooled like Cossacks,
hold their men, sides lined in felt,
setting foot to the frozen sea, cracked and crisp;
a prairie of ice.

Nubile cadets brace their bellies,
binding hands bare-knuckle blue,
ready to skitter, light as a fly,
over cold leagues of maritime distance,
like Shetland to Faeroe.

The freeze seizes
their hopes to come,
and at the end of the ice,
reminds them who they wanted to be.

Some will skate, and some will shimmy,
and those who long for home,
toddle their way back,
before pale cities,
before cold memories
recede too far
to find again.

**Wyoming Traverse**

Jumped-up in lumberjack check
stockings sure
with palms in pursuit
I rove unbuttoned
slack and loose
between instant looks and curly smiles
my sights settle on a buckshot muse
her fasteners secretly tight
devoid of foreign fancy
when her eyes first fluttered true
and wrinkles found form
a line of sky painted me blue

Tanked in togetherness
flywheels ran fast through downed fences
our bouncing countered the ruts and splits
as we curb and reel the posted roads
at diverse angles
through thin northern lips
I am inhaled in silent capture

The gripping pleasure flew loose
from my jello'd bones
an afterword was there but not spoken
and as sparrow and bee can be kind to each other
it would only take half a glass of thought
and a shot of reason to know we are
lobed halves of almost the same
flecked and fleeced like the wild
and that

Somewhere in front of my name
is that flash of blue

## crosswalk at 7<sup>th</sup>

wearing city tuff I bite down
champing at brick and curb
toes searching for grip
in overstretched shoes

pure as this corner
ninety degree fine
taxis in dim alert
pull over unpaved puddles
hinting yellow
for girls in boycuts
cropped close on the morning side
and wedding guys alright in stripes

subways trundle near
lights change
in hatted blur  I chase exit
losing track to lazy faces
pigging in with doubled knees
then drift wide to wiser lines
displaced by the same shadows monuments made
before the century

trading day's
imperfect sums align
blend and strobe
giving me chin mid-step
to fit into a story between pedestrian paint
with simple steps
to trace the switchbacks life takes
some twisting thin

midtown rabble sours the air
I look up
trip tight
and roam alone
into my blind beyond
the sidewalk's edge
dunning my soles

## Le Bal

Cubic blue prisms the ceiling,
twin hips twinkle the dance floor.
I grind my soles alone;
poor margins at cuff and shoe
wish for higher legs and lighter toes.
Nervous feet pimped for a rodeo
slide around me in two's—
I am margarita-miles ahead.

Cosmic eggs round the room,
megawatts boss the charge.
Bouncing like bloomers of the *Folies Bergère,*
we are dancing dogs with painted tails.
Jersey Smile in Zebra Shoes wide-arms the bar,
pig-knuckle dumb; cracks a look
with a side hip shift
to run the rooks away.

Life is dotted in diamonds,
disco lasers scream through second-hand smoke;
adult drinks load slingshot sting.
We are B-24s rumbling over flak,
children with the sillies,
roaming bones with ghostly stares
under strobes that blind the night.

Floating rings twist and twirl a candied court.
Mustang Eyes in Cherry Lips
shores her shorts to the high water line and wades in;
backbone follows what lumbar learns—

we pace light as running hounds,
*ta ta click, ta ta click,*
ankles tangle,
and after a backstep delay
we torque, jaws tilt—
some kisses stick like lipids,
others dissolve to air.

White blossoms pom-pom the walls,
bands of others pound and push;
Jersey Zebra casts a loaded glow.
I take Mustang in a brave squeeze—we bind tight
as I imagine a shaking sable in my arms,
cradled from a backhoe crush.
Through late night jukes,
the spin is spun.

Under bleach-white closing light, shadows get shy;
the room now a bus stop for wobbly oranges
and unpaired warblers who bob and blink
and back their necks away
from every half-tone hustle.
Mustang is by now my junk partner,
her breasts like rising planets—
travel bunnies to the next bar.
Jawbone loud and sawdust rough
in a crow's gait we crawl,
*ta click, ta click,*
*ta click.*

## I watch your window

from the streetlamp
that duels the moon
one single summer night,
planting guesses
at how tarnished is your pillow,
how deep the dust
below your bed.

I watch your window
a few times more than often,
to await the bait
at shallow depth,
luridly close,
of a sudden curtain's flutter
from behind forward dormers,
under shingles' perfect pitch.

I watch your window
while a twist of willow
screens you from my private eyes,
as I study the fold
of your fingers
when they pull
the shutter latch
close.

## Mogador

where ripples mosaic the bay
seagulls cry and klaxon
not to echo the caliph's call
but to ask why I lumber low
a heavy boat weathering to port
coasting to belay my weight
to the herringboned quay
where mapmakers wandered
whispering a lighter language
in airstreams of sound

will I
break through the drab
all noble stars cross
stretching over dunes
dull as cold copper
where mountains lord the horizon
like great stone houses
and turbaned riders pose tall as trees

this will be my way
they say
not the bad roads from Agadir
through mudded compounds
melted like sugar
but the late skies swallows swift
over tilted tiles
scudding to erase the air
of all feathered traces
unafraid to fade

## wandering for God*
*six eponymous anagrams*

### onward, go fringed
on fire treads
downy loose
in tame attire
the corners to round
will come slowly


### forgoing red dawn
morning thoughts panic
tassel tops bounce
fun fused all around
before things went snaky


### frowned, go daring
crazy as crow
erratic as flame
fly live
hard burns can go
to the back porch
for soaking


### end going forward
tumbleweeds toss
through a city of women
with their mothers' hips
and fathers' chins
cloned from a wiser strain
and wider warp
you wrote

**dreading worn fog**
you find where pilgrims grieve
at their final station
touching turf
overloaded with clover
there you stood soaked
from tongue to toe


**go and grow, friend**
my lane's the same as you
we'll do well in grey
how to phrase in lo-flo
you knew lines ago
this gate opens
further than a hinge creak
admits


*lifted from Bruce Chatwin's notebooks on a possible
book title*

## Passage

I eat what the fork can find—
drinking by bottle or by shot;
cup rain by hat, dish and open hand,
take shelter under wattled withes,
and bird my way through fell acres to seek you,
still not knowing
your face
or name.

Hagiographies grow—
you may be bright as Pleiades,
stretching light to read my heirless histories
that would scathe a grimace
or grind a cicatrix to the skin;
but conjugate from bitter to sweet in a bold say—
a calligraphic slash, blackletter bold
to end my downwind hejira
as you wander wide,
and drift like a ghost through dark wood walls.

As long as these eyes
still gleam the sport of life,
let migrant hands be landed
to reach your cheek,
frame your shoulders,
and pull your breath to me.
I will show you my jewels,
unfold my silk, lay out my silver for you,
awaiting—
armored, but harmless,
feathered, but flightless.

# 2.
# Comets riding the night

## Frigidareum

I save my obsessions
for the cold part of the house:
the gentle sting of a shaken martini—
its evaporate asking,

> *"What occasion you ring*
> *in this frigid empire of un-dusted angles,*
> *heavy porcelain, silk cushions*
> *mourned and muted in baleen blue,*
> *that exhale lungfuls if you sit?*
>
> *Why do you come to this estate of doors*
> *weathered tight to their jambs,*
> *browned water-stained walls,*
> *and a desperately overstretched rug*
> *where broken jokes and crumbled puns fell,*
> *where your uncle toe-tapped a tango,*
> *cotton soft, as the hi-fi played*
> *one summer"?*

If you must know,
this is where I come to savor
flavored lines from *The Last Dominion of Ragmore*,
its passages ribald and exact,
to devour them like midnight chocolate,
while outside the windows' slatted blinds,
winter sparrows rattle.

This is my refuge to suck
a cherry lozenge unbothered,
try to say something sunny,
and review mica samples in a ginger jar;
take roll for a company of antique dolls—
their 49 eyes witness me
off-gassing conceits.
Things I cared not for
now dwell my days.

Chilled plots for tenpenny sins
to which I will never confess,
remain secreted in my cold preserve,
saving me
from the heat of tomorrow.

## At a cafe on the Strand

Her shirt bottom sailed, flirting the wind,
and through a sidewinder smile,
she cursed better Russian than a cosmonaut
at my truant view of her laced brassiere,
a prefecture of kindness,
cupping the front of all that is right,
simple and sane.

A tentative lip smudge on her napkin
hinted a tongue plum from ruby Port;
painted toes in cyclamen pink
and eyes of planet blue
recalled a canvass by Matisse,
of a morning in Tangiers,
where blood oranges, opened like wounds,
stall the dares of lovers' play.

Hopes glide on soft feet
to nearby accordion sambas
that wind the night's wheel,
drowning conversations to gestures and nods.
My eyes aim at hers, then wander
down the folds of table cloth
to the strand's pave of migrant fishbones
and spent cigarettes.

She smartens her seams,
with pearls to please;
a loosened curl infringes the collar—
volunteer ivy about to make a run.
Blond bangs over mascara acquiesce
a back row of unbleached roots,
like a preacher who nods to the unbaptized.

Then freshly, as a blush of berries,
from what could have been written
in a battered book of a Seine *bouquiniste,*
she rises and I follow,
pulling my suit together behind a caramelized smile,
walking to what darkness waits for.

## Wake

I lie awake,
a warden of stone,
chattel to darkness,
keeping my bounds
amid tornadic sheets;
and acquit quietly
to half-knowing you,
but for the involuntary little sounds
of a body at rest,
and the meter of your breath,
chaste and tame.

It would take more
to know your midnight shifts
of restless reason,
episodic snorts
that flare the air
in dialogue with wolves,
and by morning,
an overhead arm framing your head in cameo—
still life of ecstasy
by drowning in dreams,
come weal or come woe.

In the same way your hair
un-summers through September,
our silent sides will turn about;
two tiger stripes alike,
guarding their parallel,
as I stalk the second half
of your nature.

## voyage

could I be the one
to discover the curve
of your neck
that only happens
when you turn in surprise
at a billowed curtain
full enough for sail
to embark

with no captain or crew
or belongings
except for the hairbrush you hold
knowing that before there was blue
there was blackness
then the birth of forms
the origin of names
naming yourself to what translates

as a morning child
snailed as safe in a waffled blanket
as in a shell's chamber
fair strands wisping your brow at the moment
Leonid showers shot the austral sky
birthing a wish that would fit in a paper cup
to defer the end of everything
until the night

a white twist of hair
takes an unwritten turn
beneath arm-length strokes
when the window
at last inhales

and you glance back at me
as from a new world
hairbrush loose in your hand

## Charleston

flexile as a winter heart could be
whiskey straight and soda perfect
she wears a Christian wide size
and bides by the Chatham House Rule
toothy with tongue charm
dances to the radio all night
in nothing but a slip
her mother's pearls
and a ring garnet-dark as a mine

'says we'll go down to Charleston
to waste a few days
drink the heat
and sweat ear to ear
rhapsody dirty rice
juleps and crab
on a wrought iron white trim veranda
ceilinged in breezy light blue

why not let's go says I
bursting from seamed silence
at the crossroad of curious and crazy
it's either a chain that pulls
or a rod that pushes

but did you know
when I scuff up the stairs
sanded smooth by rough soles
to your upper stories
feeling cellophane light
as private prisoner to your ripstop soul
my mind retires

suddenly sewn into your hems
it would take a newton times ten
to shove my shoulder
loose from the sill
of your pillowed promises

## On the Night of Shooting Stars

My heart sends tenders
to skim your skin in ringlets
like a skater on a frozen pond;
in thatched tracks like a beetle
across Sahara sand.

Every thing is right,
every star drops where it should;
faces lose their patterns,
fingerprints fall away—all renews.

Something big watches us
with animacy of an older world.
Is it a god being born
or two souls at eclipse,
about to detonate
from nearness?

**triptych**

when the air is embalmed
with a night sweat of lilies
and gnaws at finger ends
lend me your brown body's flavored forms
spread on a mattress
bare as a drum
to playfully plot and pose
what sepia shapes remember
before photography ever was

*


arms entwined in cursive curves
we two aloud in love
bind and bound our lines
vectoring close and closer
to share the same air
cleaving bosoms vent heat
heads tilt squaring degrees of recline
to study the grammar of stars
beginning with alpha
then reckon our distance again

*


after un-laundered thoughts have broken air
delicate portions of lemon and milk
measure our waking
silent symbols
renewing civilities at morning tea
forgiving the stains we make

with compliments barely buttered
to push the day forward
and once again be fleet as lovers
who gambol the curb
silly and sudden

## Cowboy Movie

By Tiffany twilight
on a Friday night scramble to the Bijou Drive-In,
where kernels concuss at the popcorn counter,
dancing like dimes in the churning fare box
of the last passing bus,

we pay late for tickets,
panicked puppets in time for entry
to see *The Last Picture Show*,
and pretend our lives in black and white,
of city pop and country guile,
before chances turn monochrome;
though home is always there
like a broom behind the door, or the dry plains wind
that plows through closing credits.

In blind rush, cars barge the exit;
headlights spear the night
and drive up Roundtop to park,
with sky so close we could pop the stars with pins.

What happens next
gets preserved like film of a western;
lit by dashboard radio dial,
eye whites lay bare
to a caucus of cicada,
fun and tumble dance to a dizzy
to be more than backseat shapes in the dark—
we are comets riding the night,
to crack the brick and dowel of cider-strict porches,
June bug-battered lights still aglow.

The feeling of wanting it all back
is tied in to your teeth,
and you keep waiting
for that bit to bite down on.

# Char

Charley:
Name for a lame horse.

Charnel house:
A hall or structure for the dead,
but not for horses.

Charleroi:
A town in southern Belgium
where the first battle
of WWI took place.

Charkha:
An Indian cotton spinning wheel;
Gandhi's divine weapon.

Charlotte Amalie:
Capital city of US Virgin Islands,
named for a Danish queen;
previously known as *Taphus*,
or, Beer House.

Charivari:
Mocking noises aimed at newlyweds,
from the Greek word "heavy head",
or maybe even hangover.

Charqui:
Is just
plain ol' jerky.

Chartaceous:
Papery, or paper-like,
but not paper thin,
like the chances
for a Charley.

## Painted Bride

Rounds of valkyrien braid
do not lounge lightly about her brow
her eyes are alive in sub-turquoise tones
with a look that could make the rain go away

She is tank-top heavy
a shouldered bosom rivaling hills
wide as heaven

Poor palms of disjointed lines
point to dangers done in darkness
as her torso harbors scars
that belong to a bullfighter

Her spine is flexed in a cambering bow
where freckles are new constellations
guiding lost mariners to the lee

Her waist is the tapering isthmus of the Americas

Broading hips for a distaff brood
lead down to the wickered digs
where thighs meet
a season's timber of beams
grained to bend
but un-kneeling

In the lower works toes align
straighter than a baker's row
and the browned bottoms of her heels
glide swiftly as barracuda

She has done half of everything once
and a doubter of most things true
yet she is plain as bucket wash
lonesome as a domino
undue for any suit
and all night floating backwards
with drifting leaves
in her backyard pool

## Lacus oblivionis
*Lake of Forgetting*

no one will know
if you haven't been
there
but if you have
you will forget
the direction of wind-
leaning weeds
the mell of marsh
sucking at the boot
as you take the long
lunge to the barque and totter
over immobile
stares of fish
their scales waxy and blue

narrow blooms
of lake grass play up
from sunken beds
where the drowned
may drift forever
unsure of their cause
you will never remember
them nor fog and waterline closing
to mute the call
from another
lost rower braying
a prayer
to find
dry again

# 3.
# On a day like yesterday

## Skī and Clef
*A Nordic fable*

As day's final fringes
dress windows with labored rays,
sober vanes assess the wind
of its own rude news: Skī and Clef,
who dwell among sanded stones on river edge,
caked in bottom silt, sally slowly
from the valley's grey rift.

They may look like whiffles of sunlight
and sound like bantering wind;
in wrinkled tune their whines pine for rot
as they gallow through your silver wood.
Steps softly scythe their way to raze your skin,
stake and hound you to your buttery ends,
and tie your rosy ring curls into sailors' knots.

Skī will leak through your cellar door
to suck the stuff from lock lid jars;
Clef will steal your eyes if they're open,
then bind your babies in spider silk
to drink the forming dew.

They will nibble the buttons from your night clothes
as you dream your arms are wooden
with hands of rakes,
shift all colors around the house,
and billy-butt you backwards
if you have not left them
a bowl of eggs by the hearth.

They will rally the rust through every hinge,
then leaf a smoky rime upon the panes
as they depart,
grey and weighty,
sullen and slow,
the tandem towing
a hollowed night behind.

## woof

i am being rused by the sick shadow of my own
second self whose hands bounce from his pitch to
my own red center churning mayhem hell branded
he barks badly from a bad batch of applejack i echo
with gilded moans then torque to a squeak erupting
floral bursts comes in bunches then bouquets on
cold tile my purpled knees slip like wet wheels in
my head it's raining stones
until
it's not
we nod
to one
another silent hunters turning home sharing heat
endure the dry grey wait daybreak his face twists a
perpendicular pout sniffing for tenancy elsewhere to
him i'm reusable to me he's disposable

## Over Terlingua

A lazy rain dangles
from comatose clouds,
kicking up
just enough
dust
of creosote scrub
to make the air
smell
like the inside
of an empty
bottle
left out
in the sun.

Then
pink
rips
a dusky
sky
in violent
hues,
waiting to happen,
before it happens,
like the
rushing
glow
of warring
worlds.

## before

before she went
tucked and bound
she had the charm
of Low Country clotheslines
colored and careless
that speckled her speech
with tiring tones
before she went

before
when eyelids weighed low
as rain-heavy lindens
of summer mornings in May
a smile was noted
close to lazy
from her eyes
a chattering Baltic blue

before she went
when typewritten thoughts
in faded ink
crowded her cranium
she got hot as a matchhead
and could raise my mercury too

she got shallow-shaped
like Cimarron Creek
with a bend of a spoon to her spine
her watermelon grin
could gleam and squeak
with lips forever kind

to the edge
of a cup
but that was before
before she went

before she went
we capered and cuddled
bathing with paper ships
sealed in soft soap
launching voyages to discover why
all drains are cast in grey

when she knocked on doors
one door knocked back
that was right before
before she went
her words got broken
grainy and grim
with the ire of a blackbird
berating the day
for not enough breeze
to carry its wing
and that was before
before she
went
away

**Only**

Oncoming high beams
pierce clouds of acacia
to graze
your face
with rough shadows,
screening summer cinema
of brittle leaves.
Fits of yucca stab the air,
alliances of luminous eyes
glare dead straight—
ushers to desert darkness.

All ahead, radio on,
a thousand and one pinholes of light,
nothing behind
but torch-red mist of tail light glow.
Swift and spanking—
you are to-night's satellite far-thrown,
to crow a fado, bellow ahoy at savior stars
over palliative V-8 moan.

And just when you think
there is something about solitude
that doesn't have a name yet,
the Roy Orbison song plays,
and happens to be
the key you cry in.

## Lacus doloris
*Lake of Sorrow*

In the drowned towns
beneath the Lake of Sorrow,
buildings still stand,
graves in drunken lumber,
where catfish drift and play
through courthouse record halls,
rows tight as church aisles
shelving registers washed white
of blue backhand ink;
everything matched
to name and number
matter
no more.

Vagrom voices
sound the names of sunken cities:

>Judson,
>Burton,
>Gad,
>Monroe,

then fade to static
as rising waterline
absolves both fortune and sin,
to erase the face
of all to make mark
in these deep parishes,
their goodbyes now less
than a wave,

or an Appalachian name
away
from sorrow.

## Badlands

The Cheyenne trail
cuts a sensible ramble
through the Badlands massif.
We come under cloud fall
within view of a pale plateau the color of smoke;
there are no bridges to broaden their beams,
nor missions to bang their bells as we pass.
This is a trip to learn about love,
where to punch a battle,
and when to run thin.

Scarred soil cracks and dry grass whistles
without kindness or contempt,
indifferent to our fates
that could dangle from the cuff of a cloud,
or curl inside the scoop of a moon.

Under folds that fetter open plains,
shadows were slant
when we swore this loaded oath,
to care for each other like broken bones,
flank our own like wooly twins
under fists of daggering wind,
and when a dozen suns roil and flare,
loosen what is no longer ours,
rough-ride these ridges 'til
night gets little, then breaks,
and morning glory twills the fence line,

banishing behind us
badlands
to exile.

## punch

shacked under
a wig of bouncing bangs
in a fit
of accidental fun
on a day
like yesterday
the kites
in your eyes
soared
in a punch
of mid-march wind

on a night
when no one died
toes tangled
hearts metered fearlessly
tall as marsh weeds
lost in a chorus
of chanting nightjars
then settled
into spoons

let me touch
a dent in the pillow
a coat by the door
a tangle of string
that says you are here
on a day
like yesterday

## On the summerteenth of June

Fahrenheit in excelsis—
clotheslined shirts hang by their tails,
with long sleeves fallen in surrender;
yet billow with wind to catch
a daring union suit
brought in by the Ringlings.

The cotton madcaps perform,
ready to die high
for e-z fly drawers, c-cups, sheets and more
until rain threatens,
and the bleached crowd
is gathered, rushed to the exit;
too soon, even,
for Hanes & Hathaway
to take a bow.

## Deluge

Speeding rain
splatters newsprint
overhead;

wilting headline:
sunny
to partly cloudy;

acrostic thoughts swim
through six-letter word
for downpour;

classifieds drip:
lost, one sure-handled
black umbrella.

## Obsequy

From the hollow closet beneath the stairs,
I reach for a suit, not charcoal, but late grey,
jacket saddled over shoulder frame,
slacks doubled at crossbar,
where above-the-knee might be.

Bachelored wire hangers bangle the rod,
tinging like chimes unrequited to wind—
lost chords in uneven keys
for the funeral of someone dear.
Church hymns will be cola-sweet,
eulogies cling to heart like cat briar.

Cut away from the half of what was,
I bow, dark-suited, underexposed,
like boneless fields of x-ray, blurry and scant,
and chance my weeping a surf of sorrow;
instead, offer lockjaw odes, borne by wool
the smell of floral scarred wallpaper.

## There

Tinted windows taint the law of goodbye
where the mist of eye is lost in translation;
mudguards wave, dealing diesel,
double-wheel treads attack the tar.

In the gravid luggage bay,
sturdy as a banker's box,
his drab duffle, dimpled and plump,
finally reclines, greyhound lazy,
below hips settled in to a seatback squeeze.

Candy wrappers stow between cushions;
he wedges between states,
in the comforting drone of the rumble zone,
to reclaim no man's land,
released from where he's been,
unknown to where he's going;
immaculate of want or regret.

Time sighs sealed in a tin,
rubber wipers flipflap miles into rain
until airbrakes release exhausted hiss,
humming and homing to rest,
and foreign feet hit the sheen of gasoline
on rain-hot blacktop.

# 4.
# Counting the kyries

## On the Night of Flies

Heat of stars tightens the sky
as the moon's blot, charged like a mighty bison,
gives glow that satyrs through leaning trees,
burnishing buzzing wings.

Bats back-flap full stop,
pick their prey mid-air to glide by
spiritless cycles of coyote dreams,
caught in the carnality
of the wind-wound swarm.

Barging like a wrack of clouds,
the insects thicken darkened downs,
flying light to ring all that ply
from *Serpens Caput* to *Serpens Cauda,*
and war the land, invading every door and window;
lining the eyes of horse and cow.

Then one-by-ten-by-thousands drop,
as if drunk from air, arrested
at the very heart of harmony,
when taker and taken,
the who and the what re-orders order,
to flatten the balance of a worried world.

Few drifters remain at daybreak;
some, unloved; others, newly brided
by summer thunder—
while the brave set course to loop the moon;
all to the last—raiding and roiling
through soft August heat,
riding high on the Night of Flies.

## DIY

A brattle in the attic
says something wild has come to winter;
I keep it at distance,
like the drip in the basement,
metronomically steady but slow.
The mirror's blemished,
spotted with blight—
its image kept at double arm's length.

Shrunk and shy
from rough sums and their get,
spirit sags when quandaries feast and fatten,
welcome as Monday.

The comfort of evasion
gives short sanctuary,
where face hides
from mottled reflection.
Barely breakfasted,
I await inspiration's gentle waff,
map strategies fast,
rumble and stilt to new convictions,
shouldering motions
to the sound
of a leak
*molto lento.*

## Le sacre

Where sunlight sustains,
visible, but impermanent,
like a smear of chalk
down Parisian boulevards in March,
bold cafés open terraces
to will the wit of Spring
upon sidewalk clientele,
hatted and cloaked in finer folds
than faithful wools forsaken that day.

Their colors, new and muted
as soft beaks and tender shoots,
gestate beneath red awnings;
half-persons speaking in minor
become whole, intoning major,
though shift restless at their tables,
like roots that thrust and yaw,
not having entirely forgotten
when life was yet
to be green.

**Pop!**

In the marches
between cowpens and wood,
the low, grey weasel,
both king and curia of the hedgerow,
provokes his corpus to bend and wind,
benign to knobby tubers
that rib his bosky corridor
in the warp and woof of the vale.

Pithing feathered prey to the furcula,
he brightens his bite
with higher tooth,
as gristle gives way to bone;
claw-pierced earth and pivoting scuffs
engrave the dominion of his world
that never wakes from its damping chill.

Dumb, in pre-horror,
black squirrels skittle the verge,
unseeing,
unknowing
of the low, grey weasel,
sticky-whiskered jarl of the downlands,
who, like them, enjoins nightly slumber,
curled for comfort,
in the shape
of a perfect
Q.

## Interiors

Chairs and tables
draped in frayed pale sheets
meant only for this,
transform my world to clouds
peaked like ice cream mountains,
meditating snow monkeys in steam-hot springs,
or Halloween ghosts in Thorazine fatigue.

Old skin keeps a log of worries
from bumps in the night,
worn scars narrate life in annulations,
never enough sun.
This palace of looming bergs,
with surrounds of scuff and peel,
itch legacies that cling.

How permanent now their erasure,
how probable these walls telling tales at all
through scraped and sanded satin veneer?

Let lines of age rule and reign
and dropcloth lift like mountain mist—
newness comes but once.

## Oceanus procellarum
*Ocean of Storms*

Merchant wrecks, liner tragedies,
and dismasted man o' war
mark debris of boatswains' graves
in the Ocean of Storms.

Mariners' maps chart

>   *The Trumaltis,*
>   *The Malibray,*
>   *The Nuncio;*

hulls a-tilt,
showing ribs like starving men
under claim by conch and coral.

A compass, mirror,
dinner fork, and buckled shoe
preserve at basalt bottom,
where eels live in greed,
hoarding boodle
for which they have no use.

As squalls rule above,
does peace reign below,
in the purgatory of all
to never hail port.

## Amtrak #291, Single Passage

She rubs the cold away,
then speeding past tilted
gravestones of churchyards,
dead squeezed tight in their lots;
gestures the cross on her breast
because that's what her mother did.
A rack of ice shelves the shore;
tufted tops of wind-bent river reed
lunge like high-hat hussars to the track.

The dark, still streaks of the Hudson appease her;
a silvered sycamore reigns the far bank,
lightning-struck tip splintered to a barb;
there a bird perches, solitary asterisk of winter.

In a middle patch of distance
the High Bridge at Poughkeepsie broods,
scaffold gateway to the grey.
Sure of nothing but the milk of her bones,
she looks up, thinking
she might disrupt the pattern of light on water,
should her body fall to the flow below
that ripples south to Newburgh.

At the trestled passage of break or remake,
her wits gather, tight as pleats of her woolen skirt,
to outweigh the valley's valence of sorrow.
Shifting sounds of signal bells
translate to new declensions—

tracks will switch, doors will open,
platform's riveted pillars flicker faces
of waiting strangers;
the place she will lose herself
to the where and now
of new air, winter thin,
stepping out until found
by what is known
as home.

## Go North

I want to go north,
where nobody cares how you look
in the cold,
and some people call you by name;

where frigid air makes sound brittle
for discourteous words
to fall broke
before reaching the ear, and
good ones suspend in breathy clouds
that thaw
in the trap of your hand.

I want to go north,
where soft and hard can meet
in solid state when wheel
atones to tundra,
as the haul pulls clear.

I want to go north,
where eyes are solemn and faces plain,
and a season's love can distill in the dark
before the cork twists
to squeak in
the light
of spring.

## Out and back

Slow sun butters down,
sinking arc of helium gold,
baring flares at angles acute
to low-lensed eyes and razored face.

What round reason be,
shooting beams from the hip
that blind my westward way,
but for late rays to pave path homeward,
wickering the street
with shadow's charade at curbstone,
onto what will be
yesterday.

## Rome

my dear long
my dear every
before whiskers lose their pull
and I am down to my last salts
I will move to Rome
and dine every night
at nine
drink in disproportionate measures
after which hour
the tags will get loose
and tales get large
you will be *ma belle*
and I will be your biscuit
you will double your lipstick
neat as a buttonhole
my hands will sway
to give coat tails
a breath
before I back into a chair
not there
curse from my wittier ends
while you laugh with your lungs
and eyes that twinkle bright
we will dance the travertine tile
in diagonals
discuss the oceans we have liked
survey the night stars
to debate
what their patterns propose

then I will sleep
to dream
we were in Rome
and dined every night
at nine

## Atchafalaya

Ibis stilt the saltings
through sawgrass and mallow,
and come dusk, bide beneath
the star-flowered galingale,
awaiting mud-colored minnow,
schooled in degrees of deceit, lining their lies
with a trace of truth
to evade scissoring bills
that pluck at the water like chopsticks.

Bullfrogs' antiphonal echoes
chant swampy epithets and tuquoques;
parked in the shallows,
alligator eyes retain prisoners' glare,
and remain bare to loneliness,
though dragonflies ribbon the air above,
skimming for nymphs.

Slackened oars break the sound
as my skiff drifts in silver-plated wake;
between green growing on green,
ghosted cypress stumps,
stone solemn,
absorb the boat wash
to silence my passage.

Around me, listing crickets' wings
soften chirrs of plainsong;
snowy egrets barrack
and fold flock for the night,
counting the kyries into slumber.

I slow my strokes to behold
no sense of anything more
beyond a world
that gives what grows,
and keeps what dies.

# ACKNOWLEDGMENTS

DC Poetry Workshop
Poets on the Fringe
Planet Poetry 28
Words, Women & Friends

First appearing in
*Encore, 2024 Prize Poems*
National Federation of State Poetry Societies:

*Cowboy Movie*
Poetry Society of Texas Award
First Place

*On the Night of Shooting Stars*
Arizona State Poetry Society Award
First Place

*Deluge*
Poetry Society of Indiana Award
Honorable Mention

# ABOUT THE AUTHOR

Prosser Stirling, a 2024 National Federation of State Poetry Societies multiple award-winning poet, is a native of Galveston, Texas. He studied at Lewis and Clark College, Ecole Etienne Decroux and the Sorbonne, living in Austin, New Orleans, Paris and Florence before making Washington, DC his home. There, Prosser has devoted his time to performance art, writing, music, graphic design, and corporate international relations, as well as discussing African art with visitors to the Smithsonian. He is a member of the Texas State Poetry Society. Other alibis include being a carny across Western Canada, apple picker in the Pyrenees, au pair in France, and marathon runner. He speaks four languages, studies Ancient Greek, and has visited over 35 countries.